HᵁMᴬN

January 2015

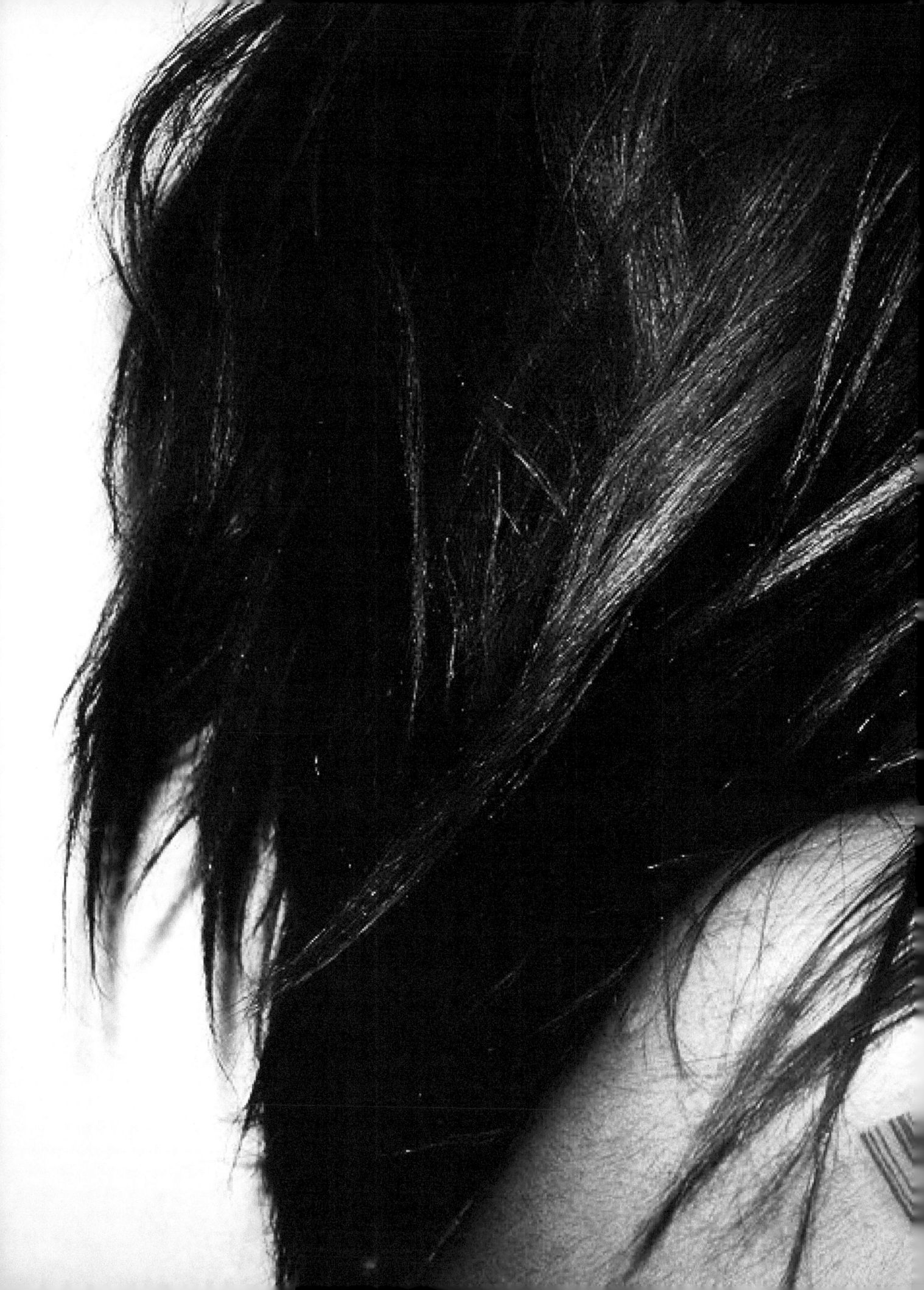

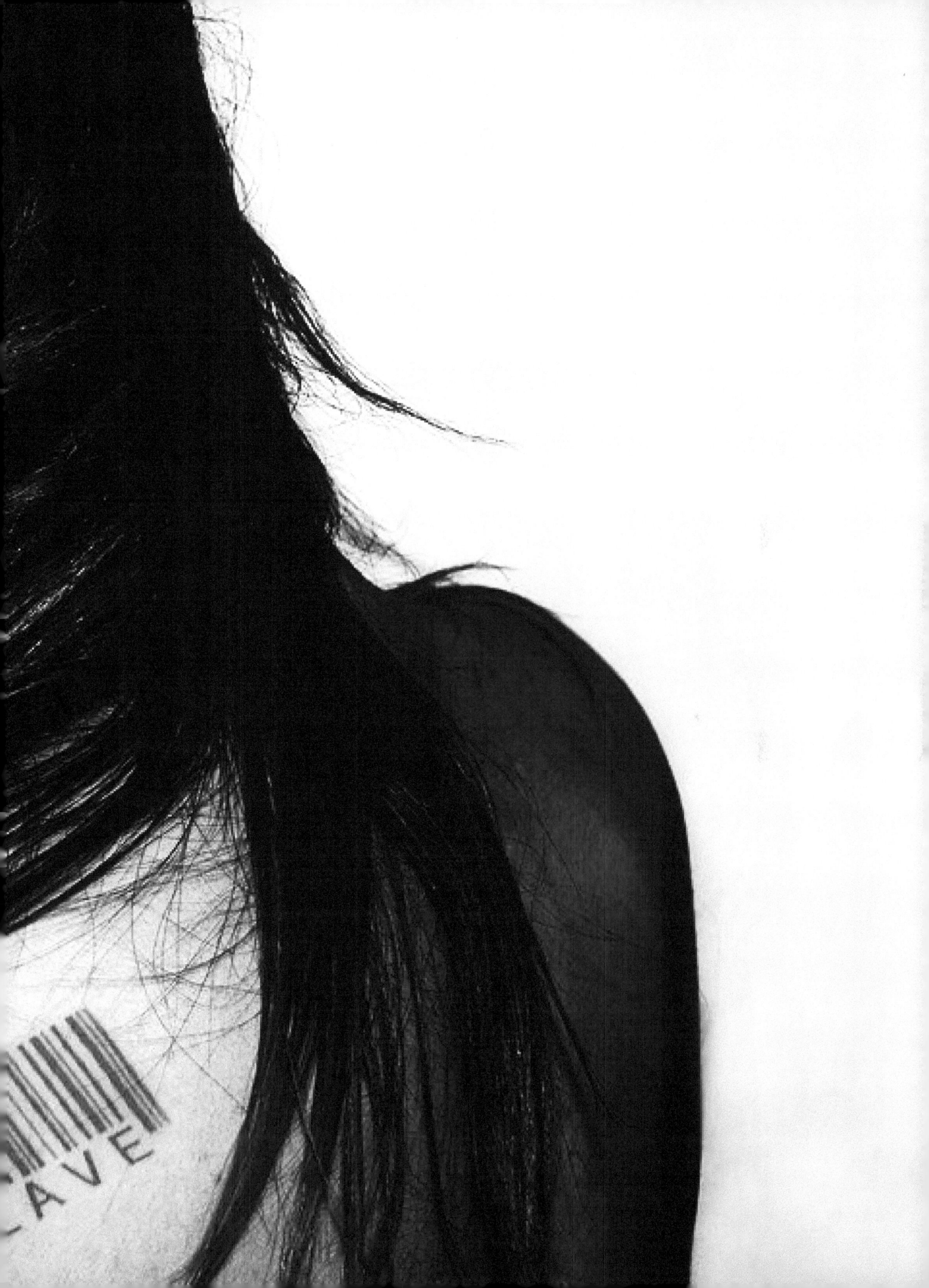

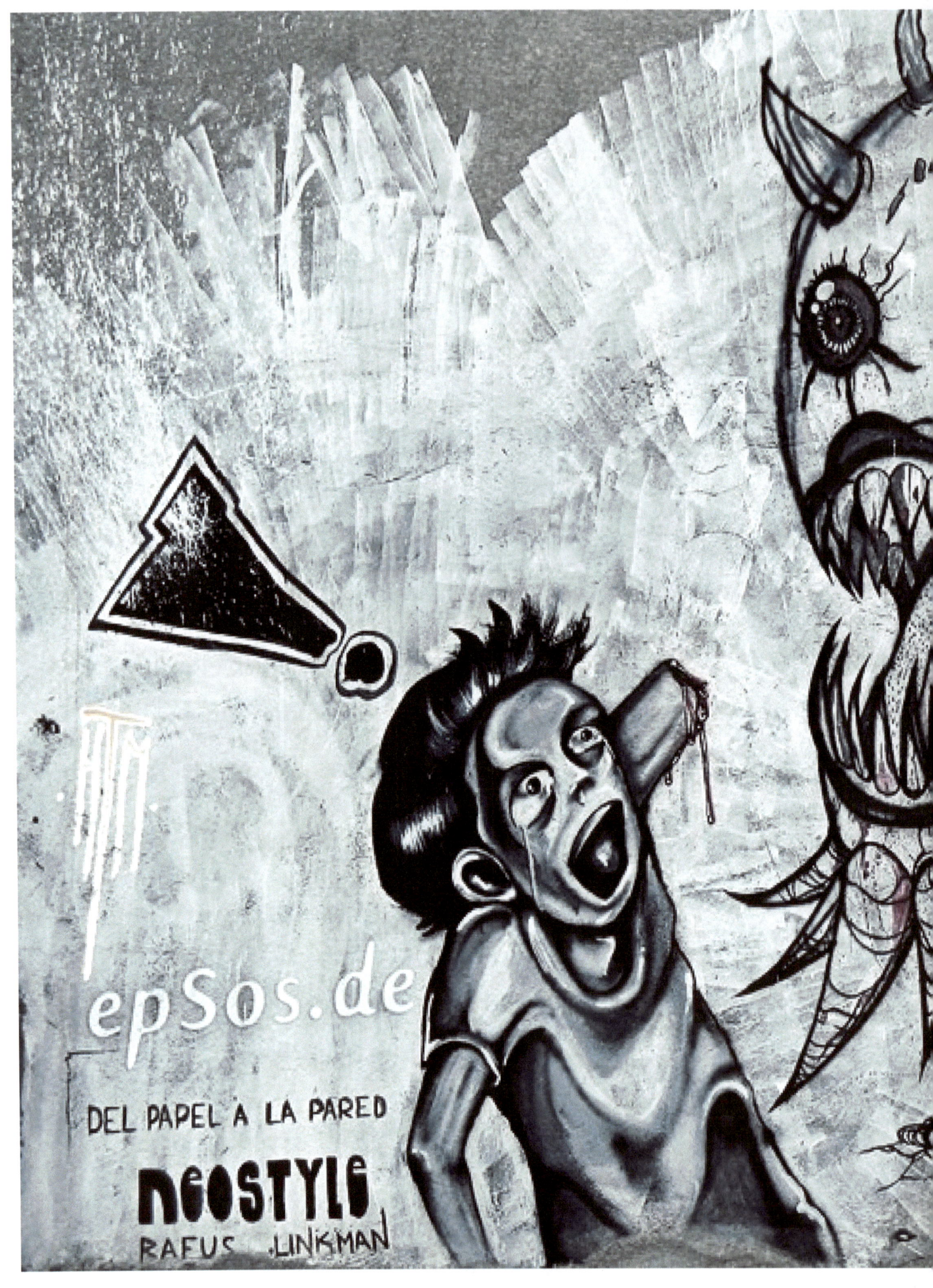

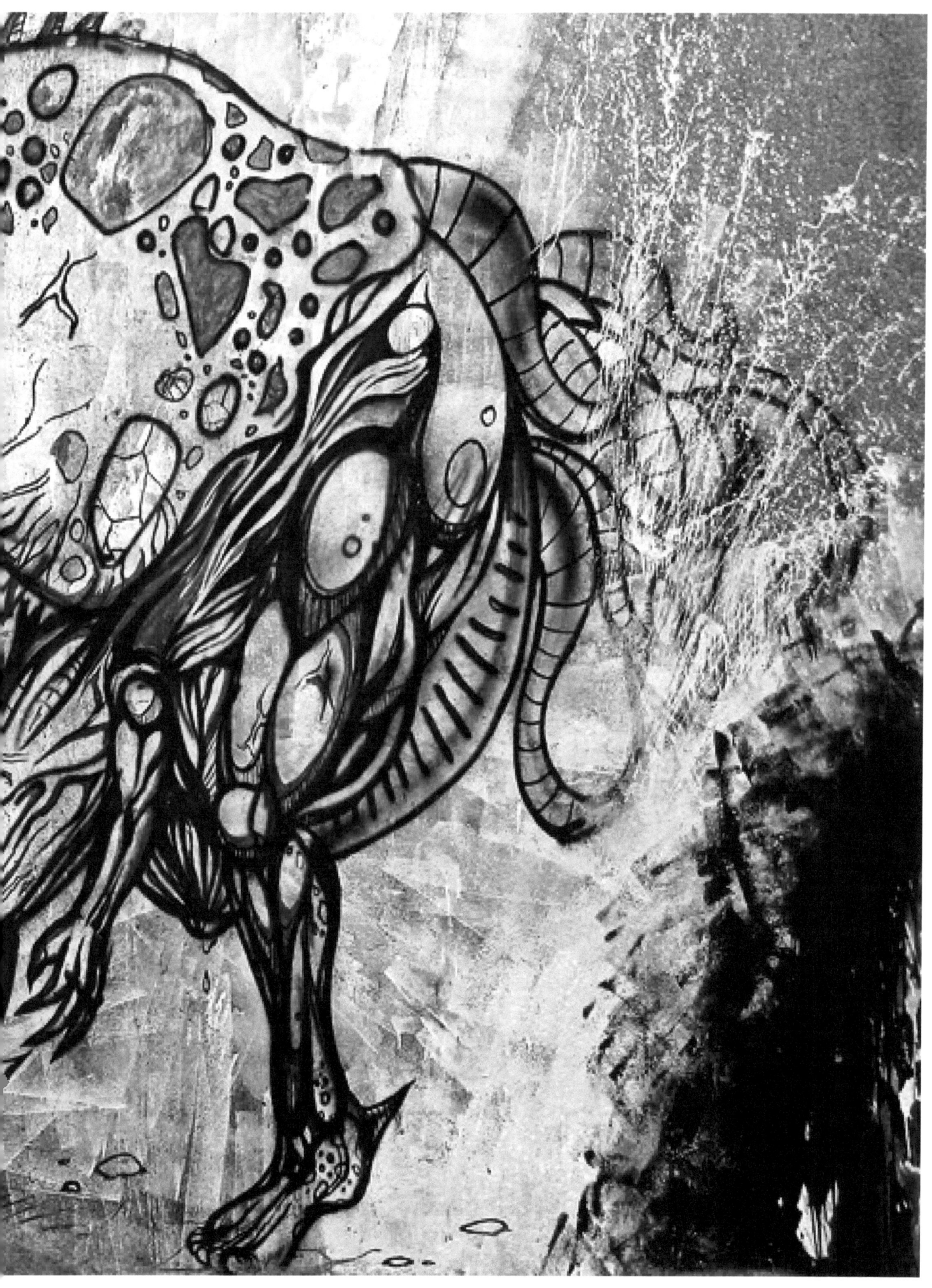

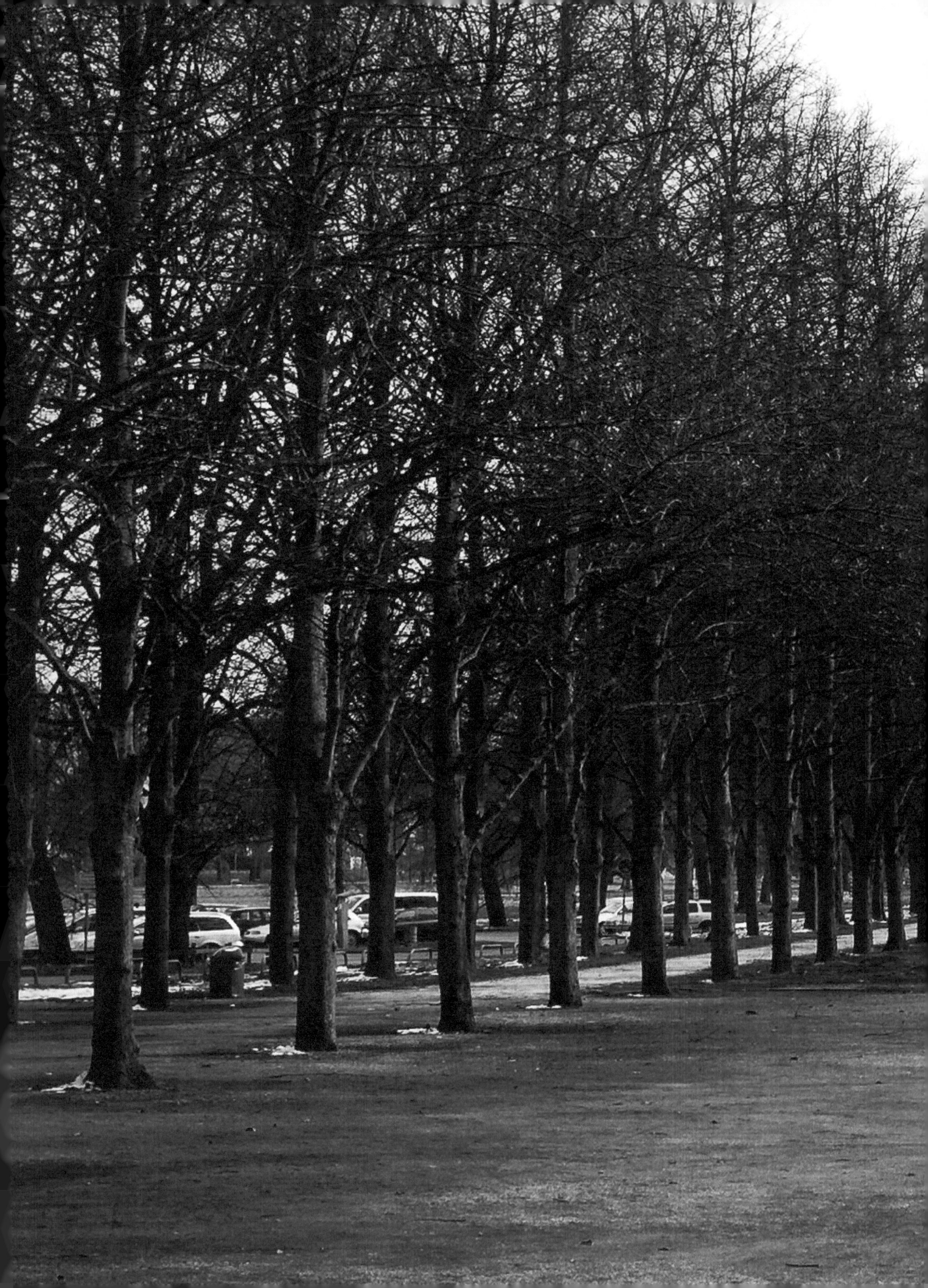

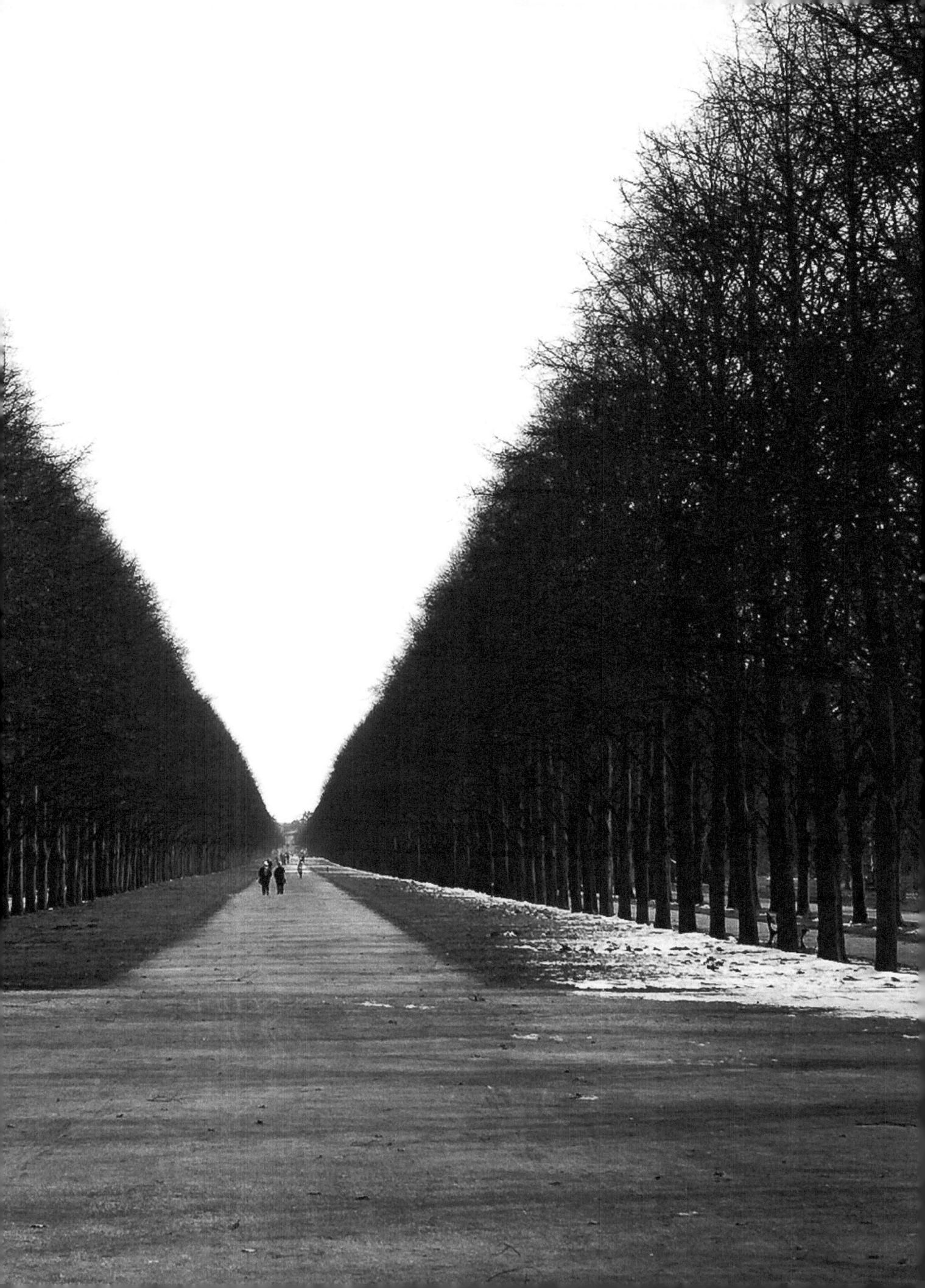

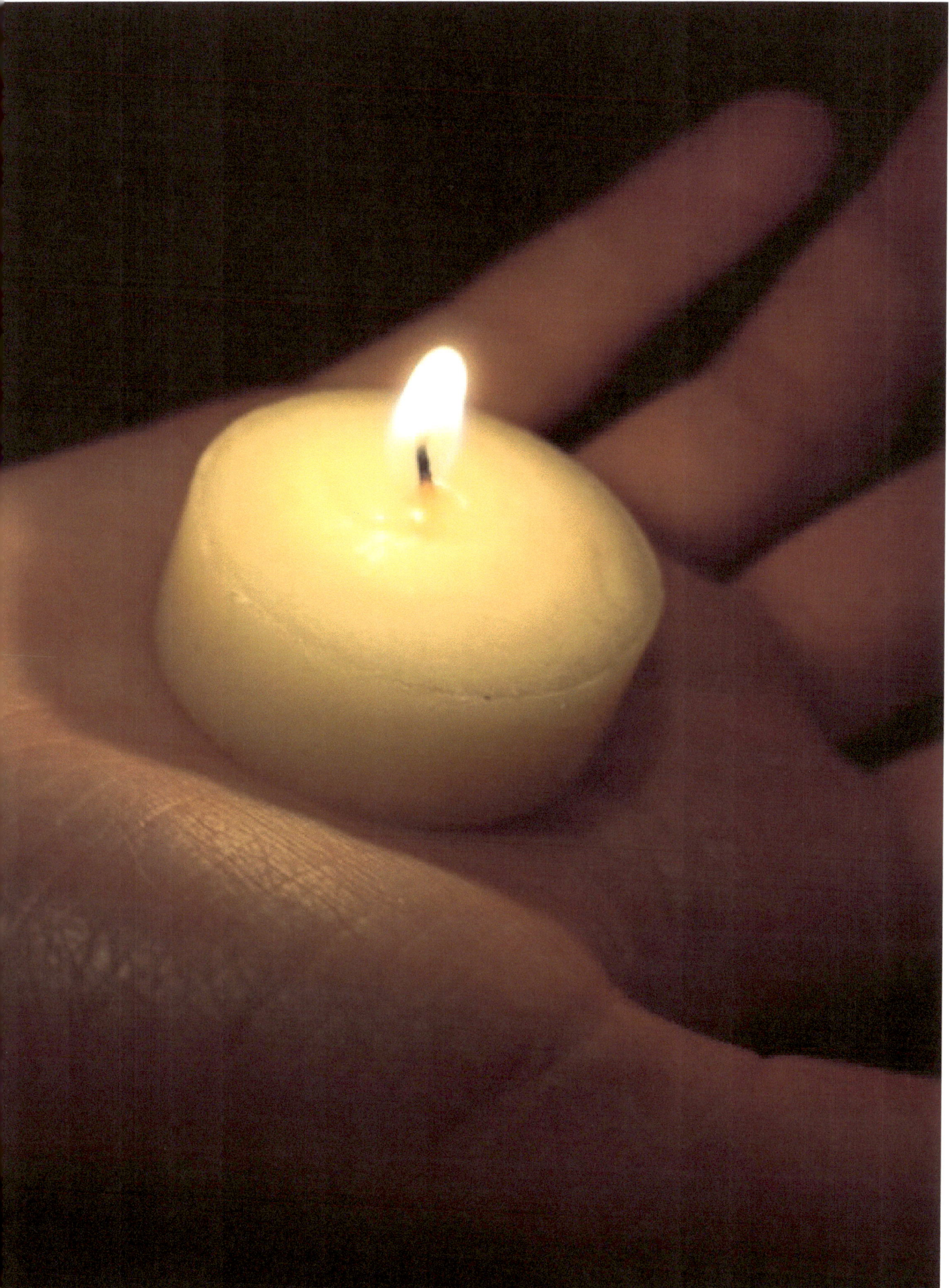

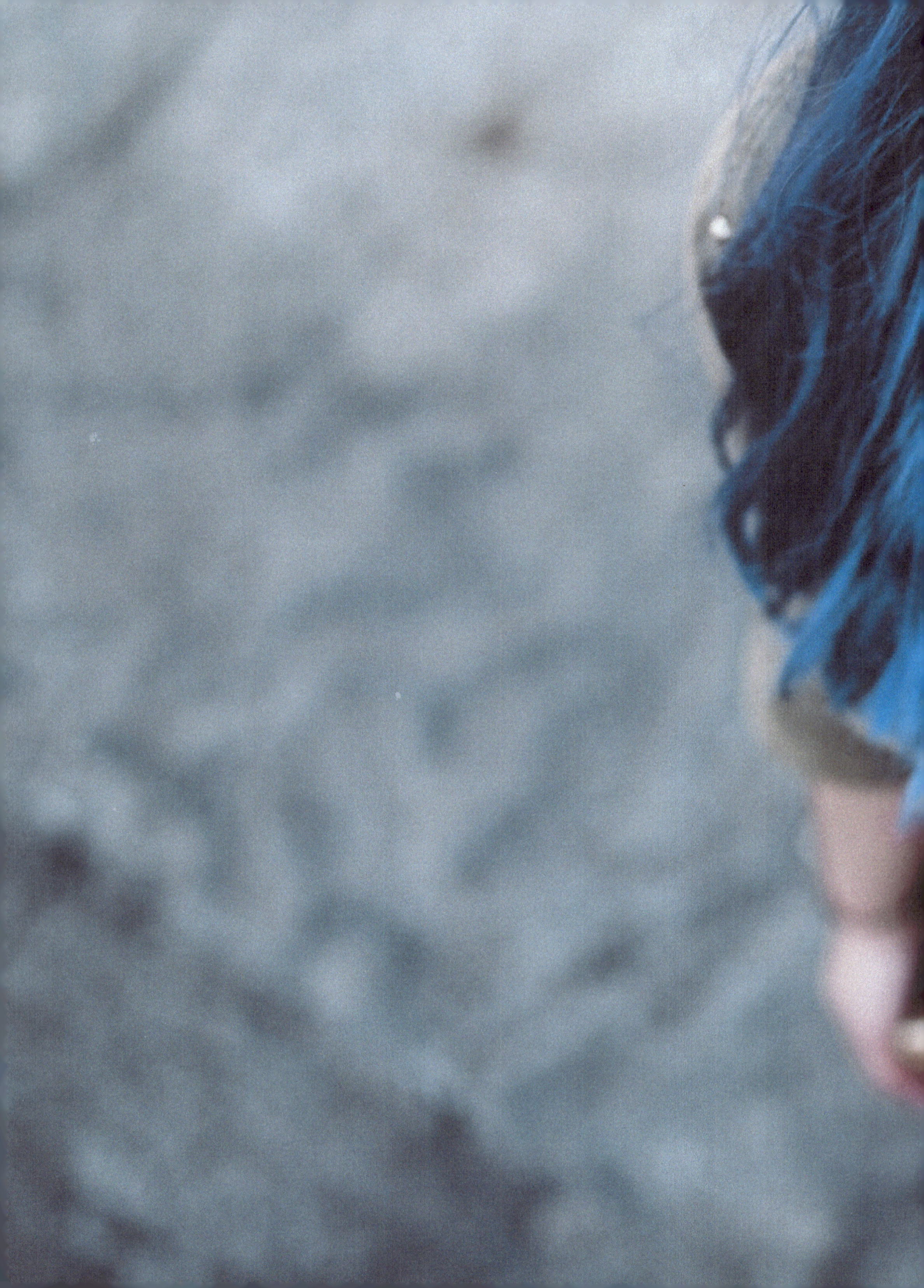

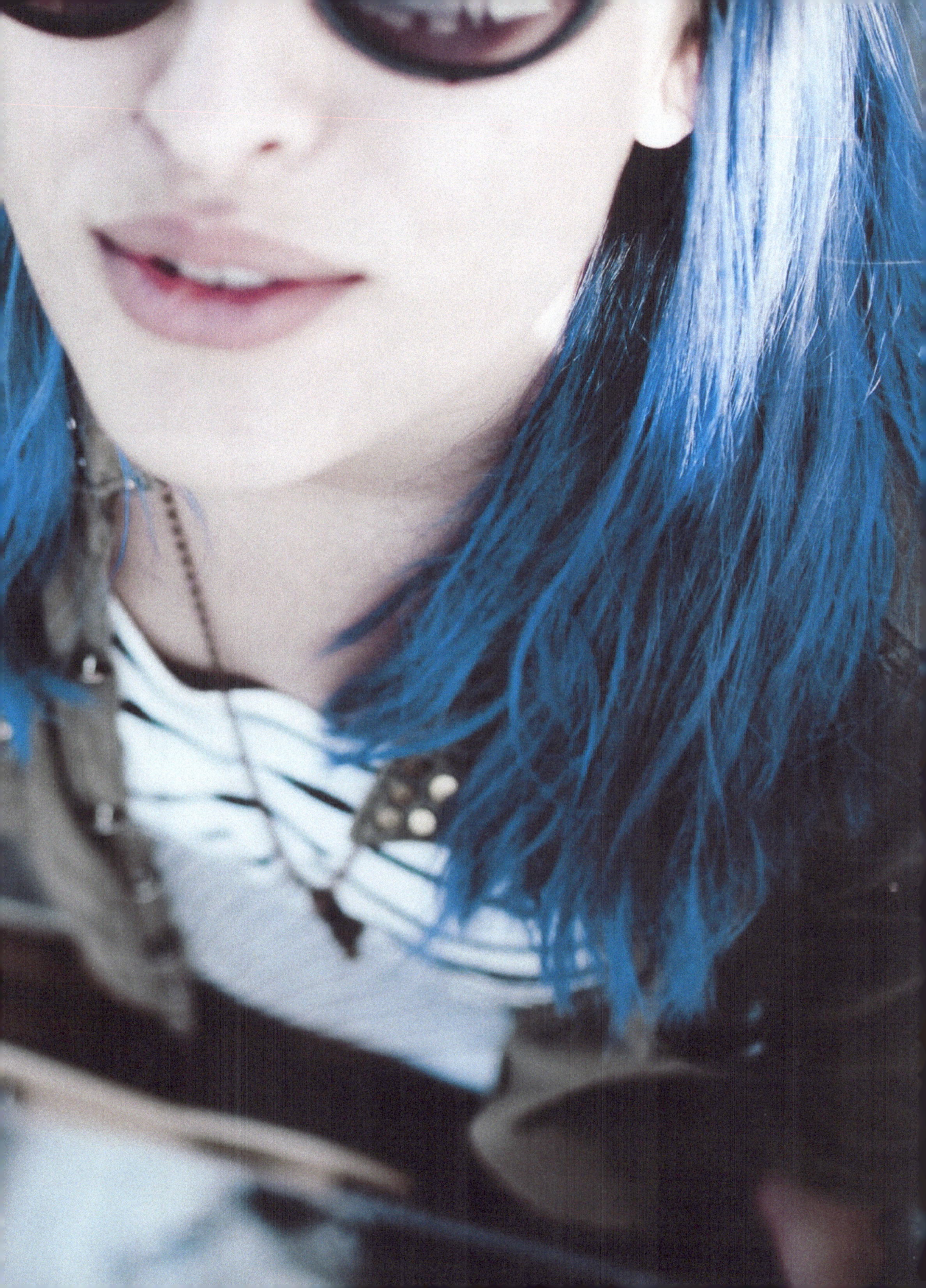

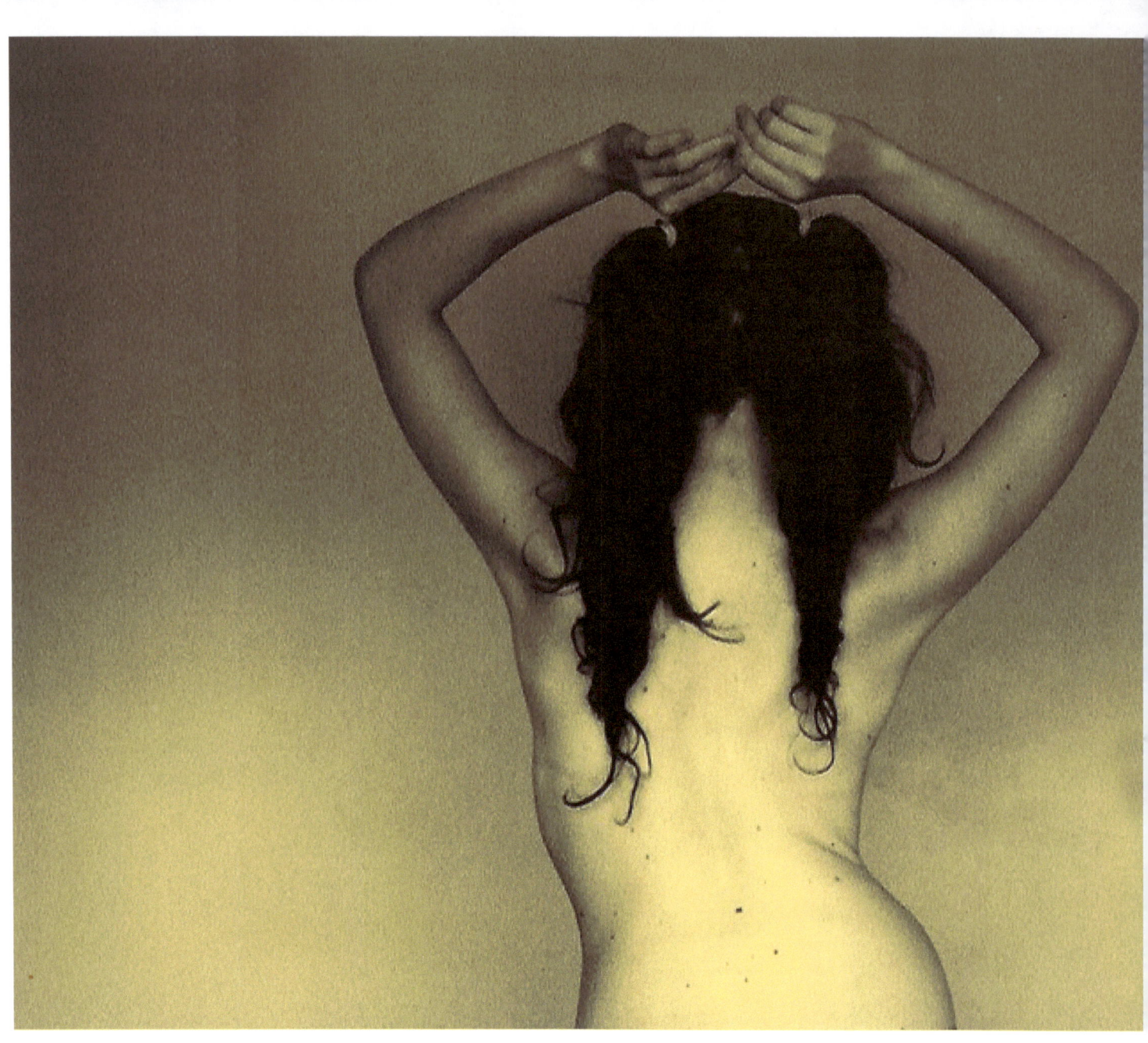

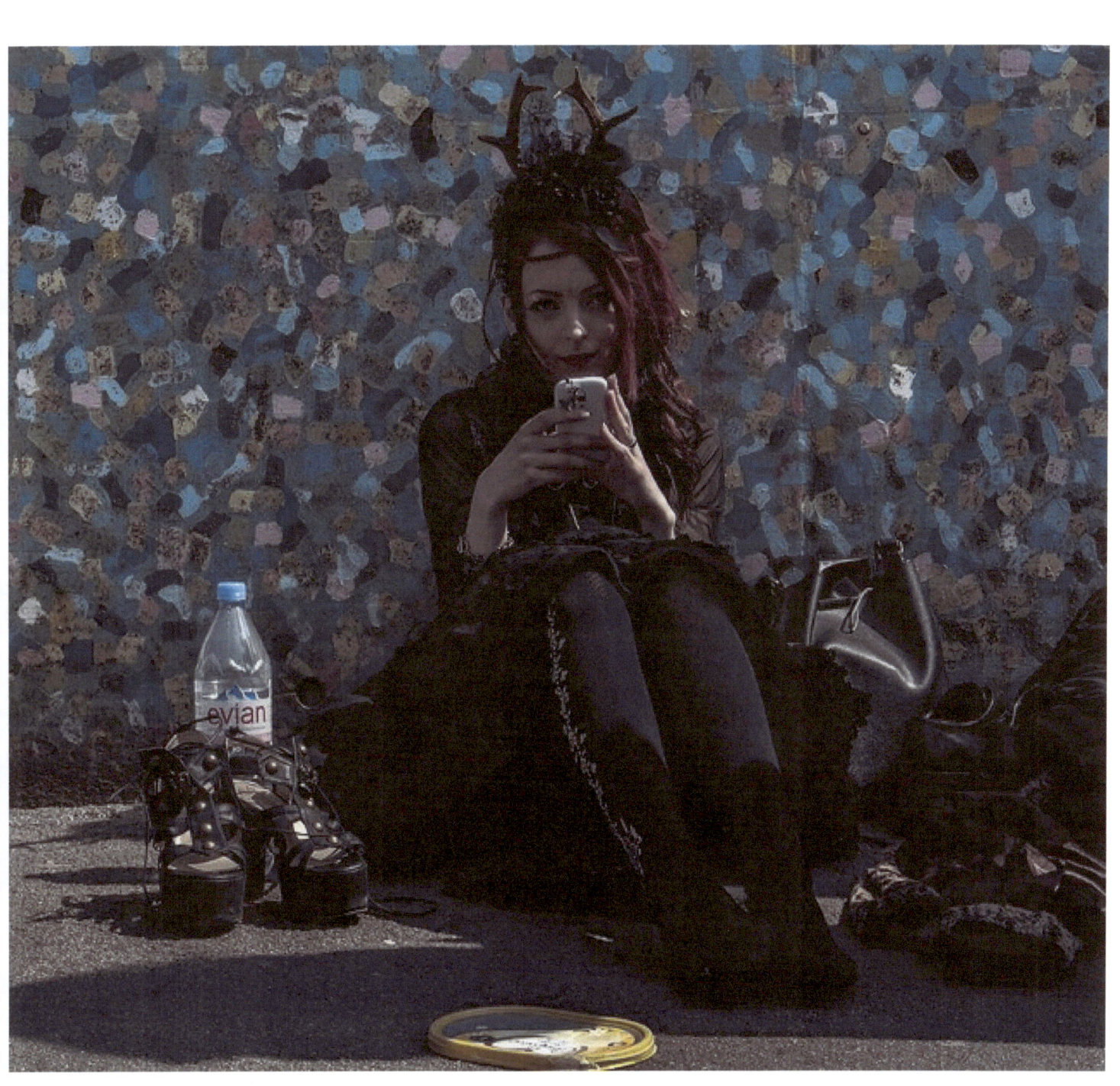

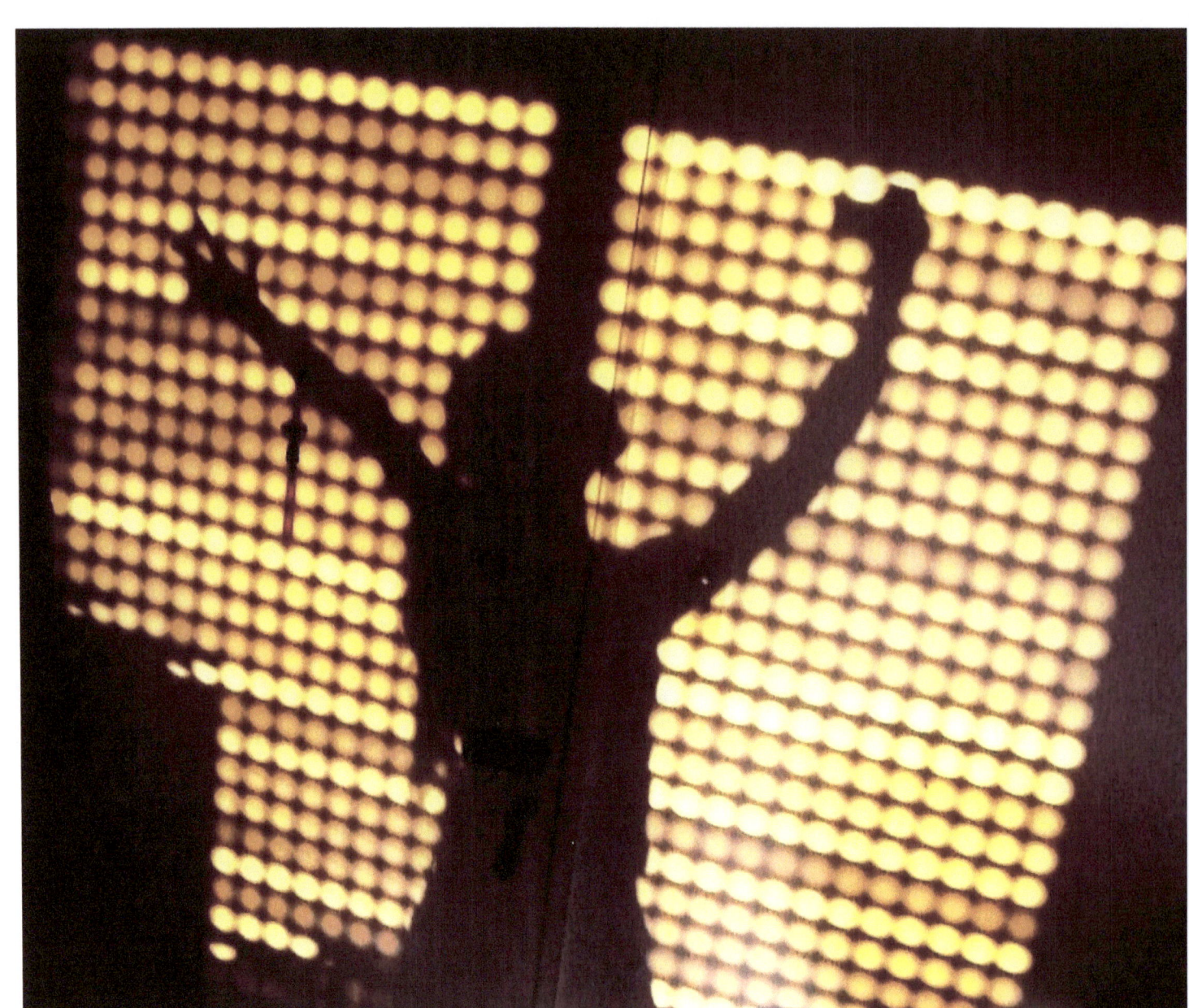

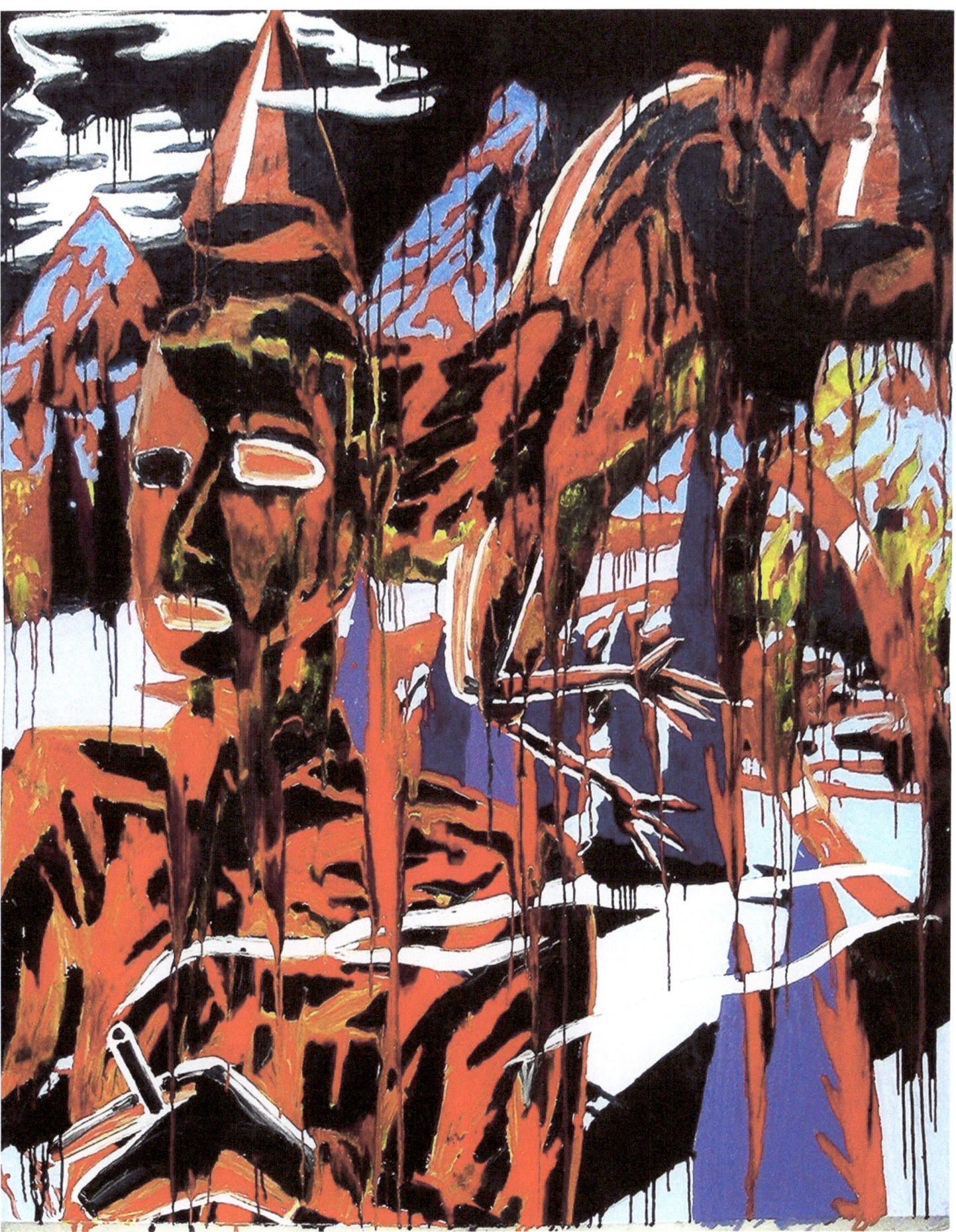

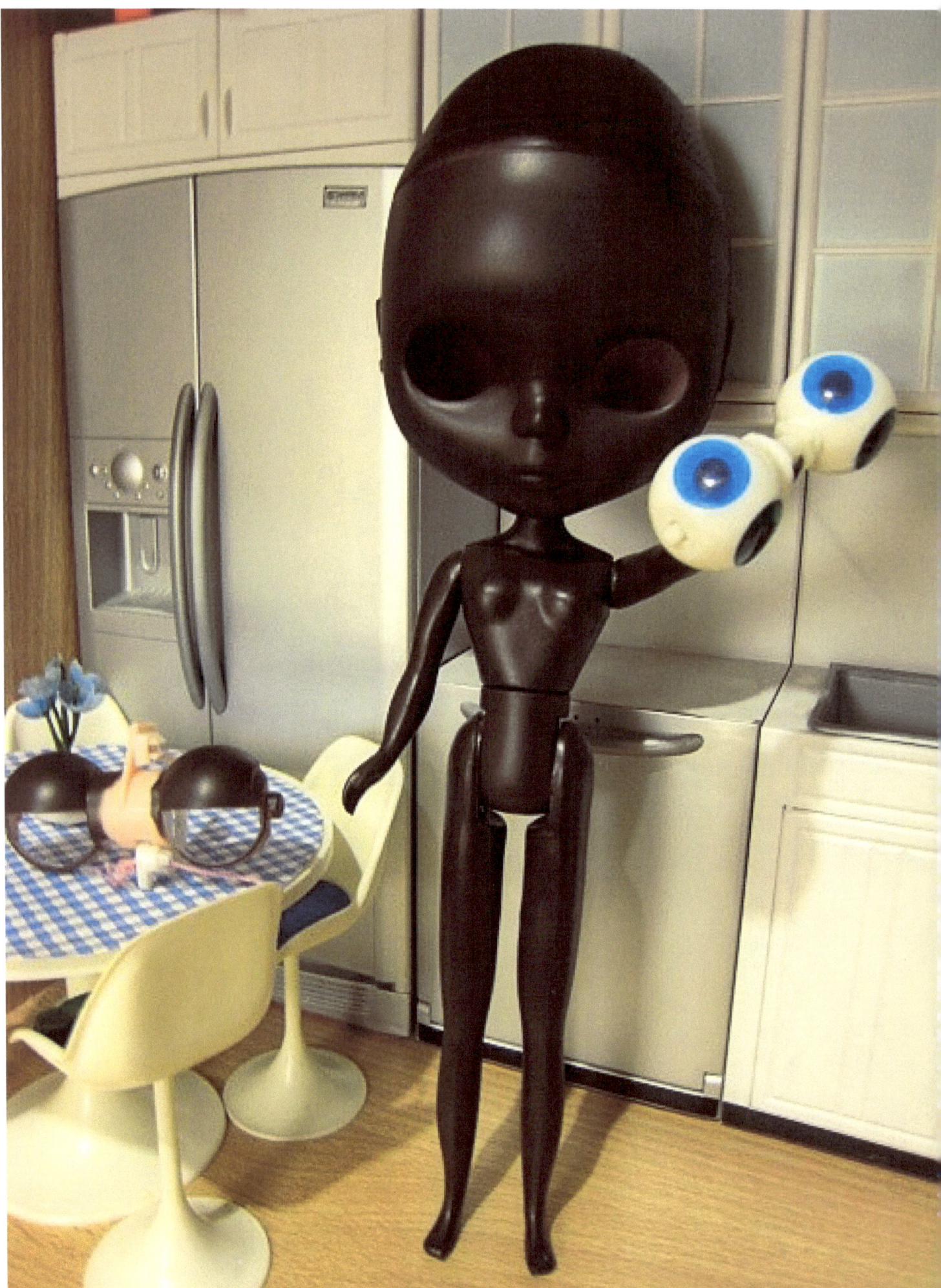

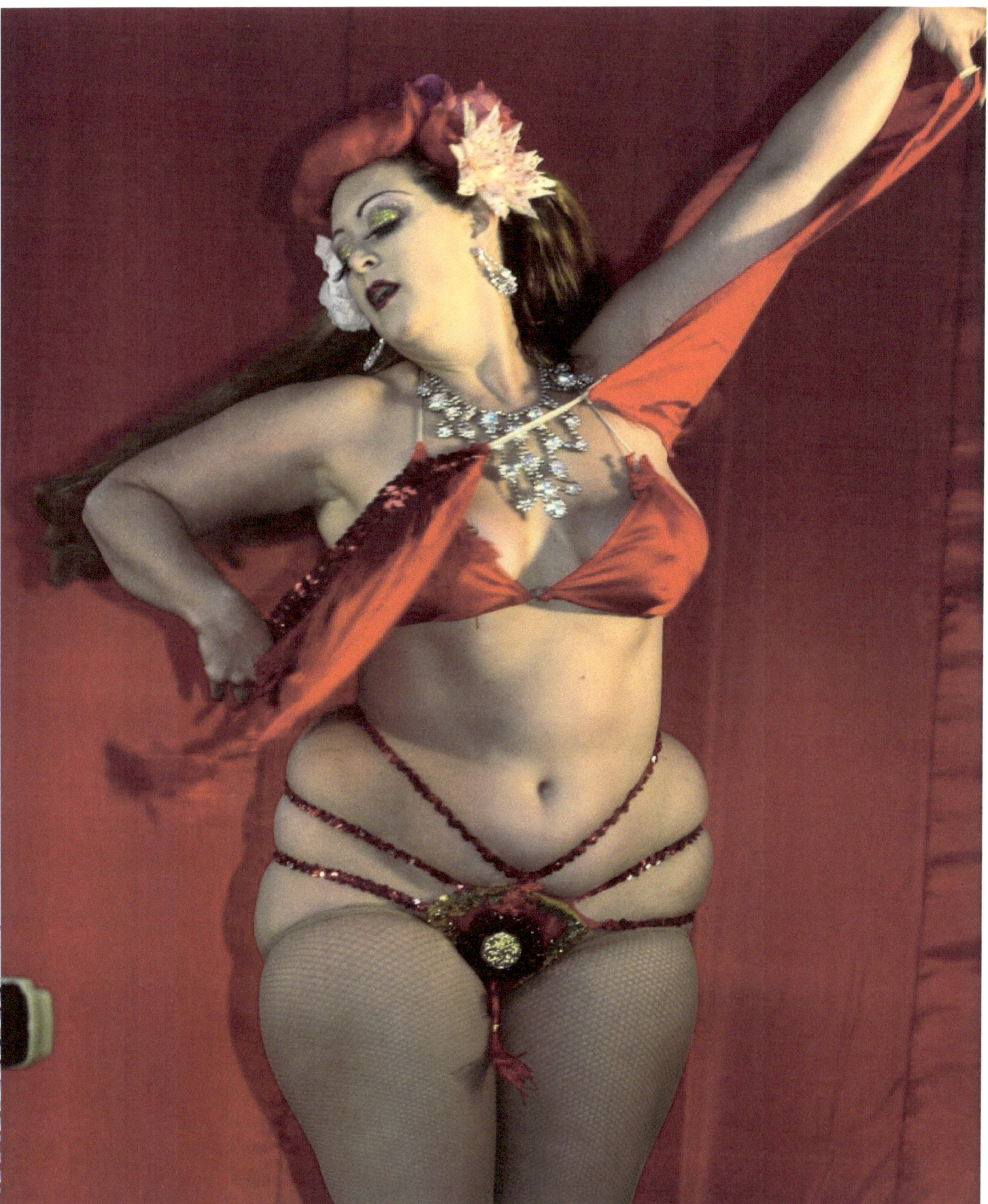

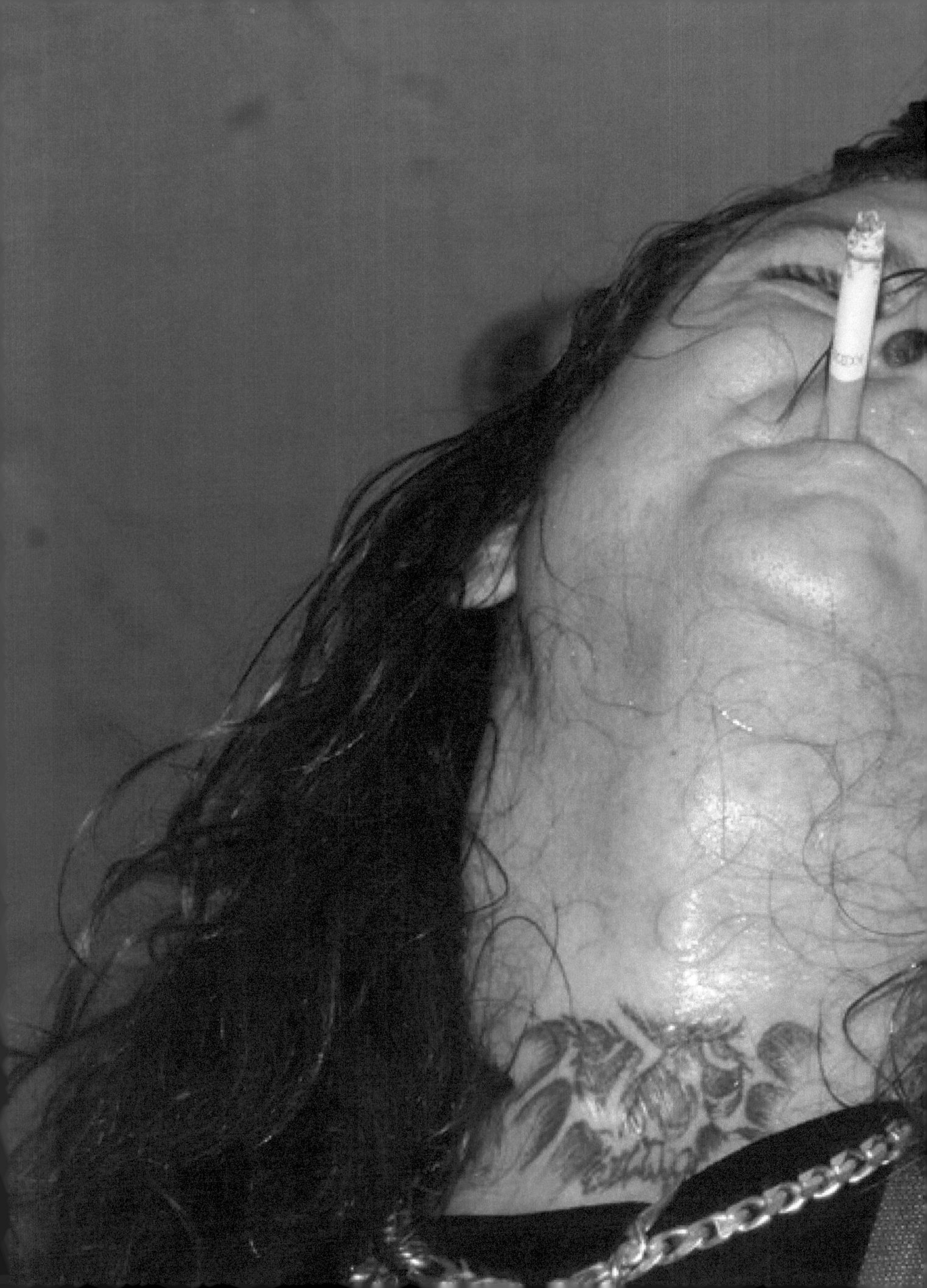

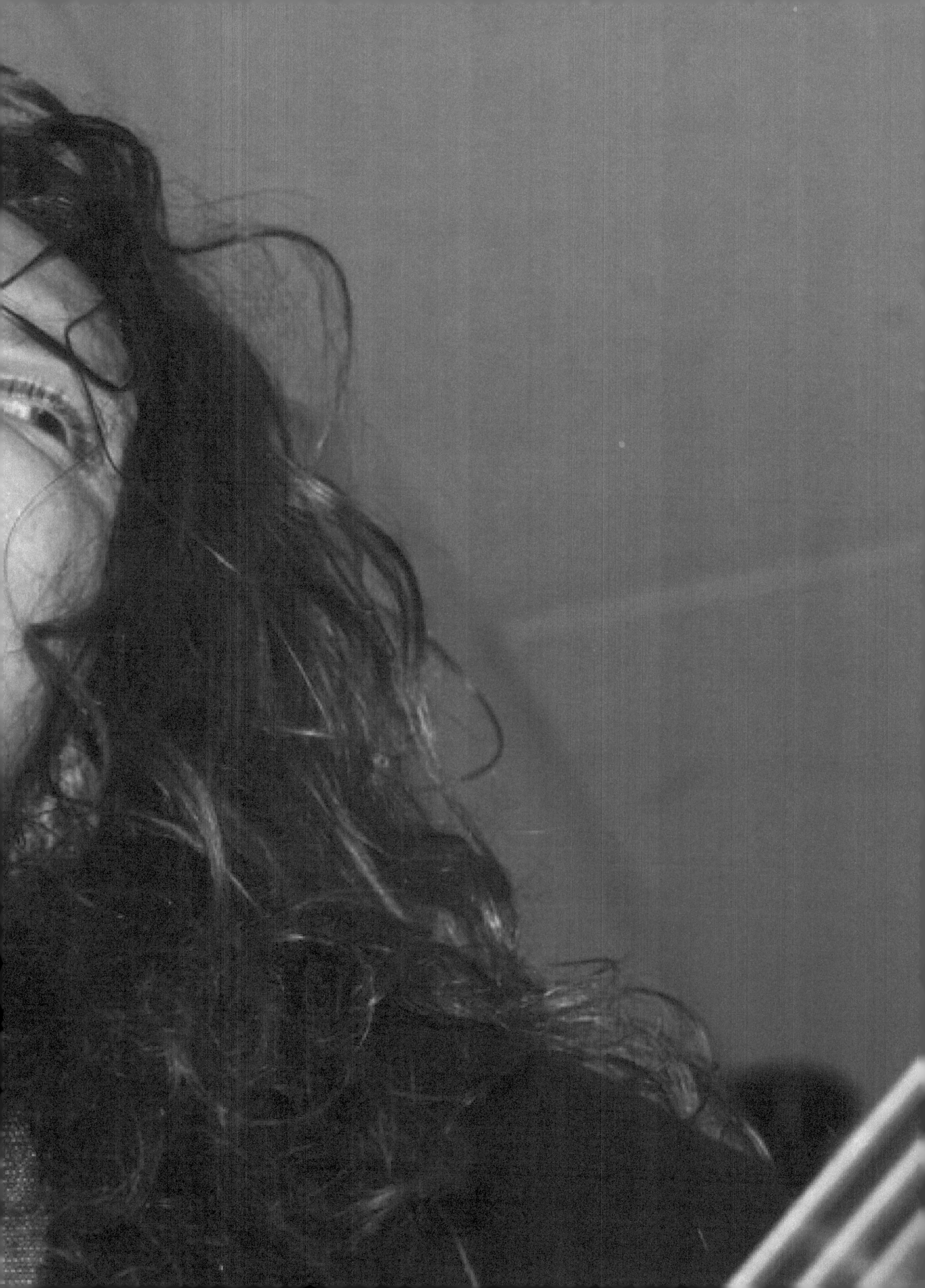

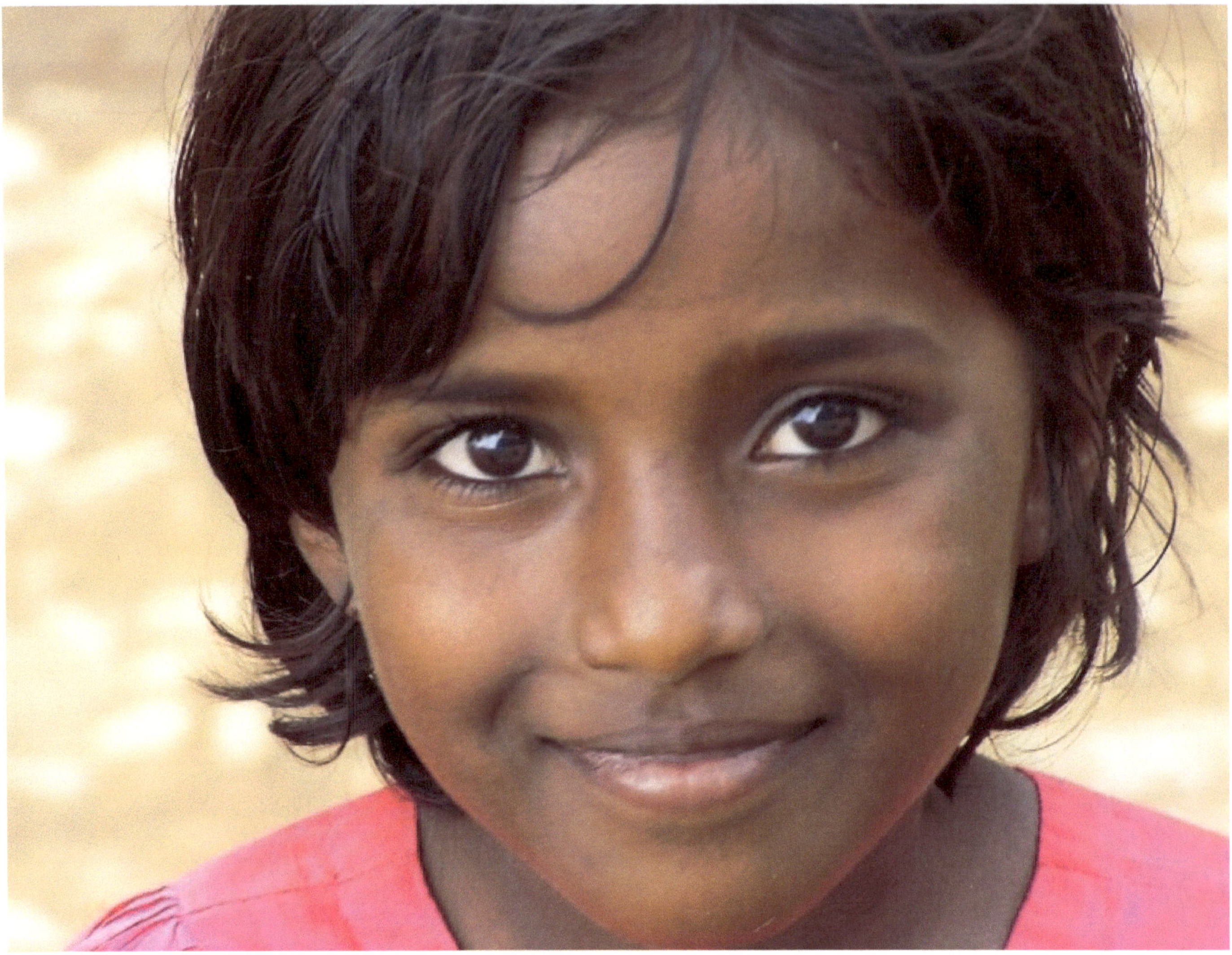

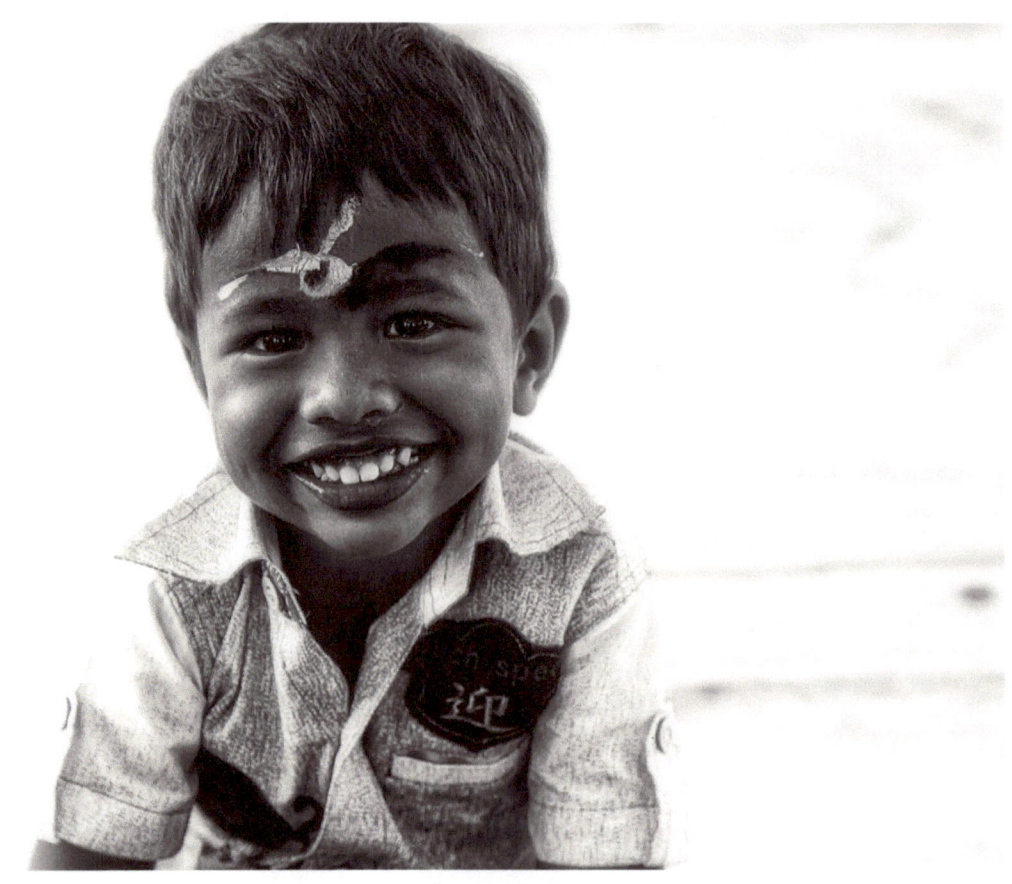

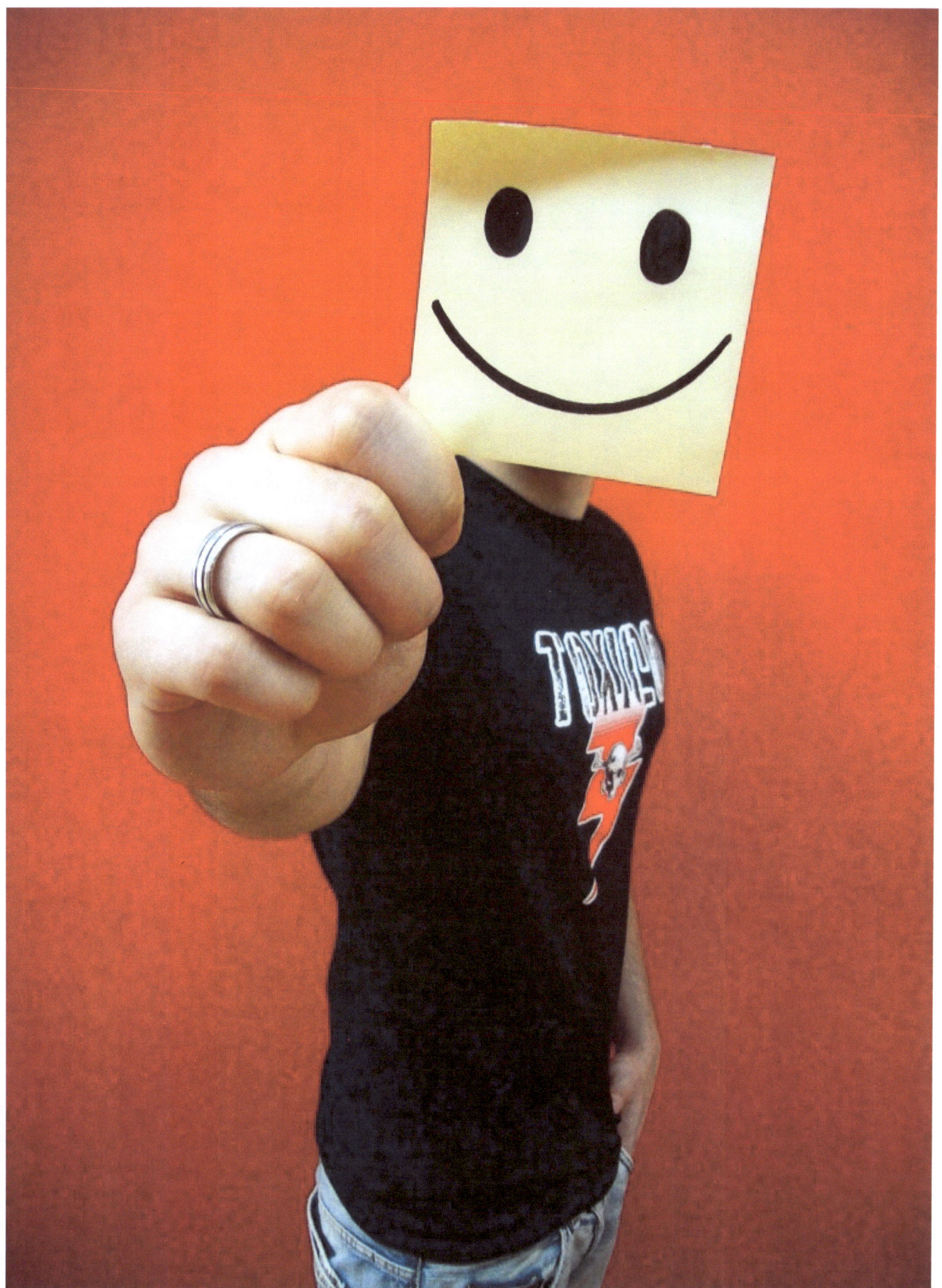

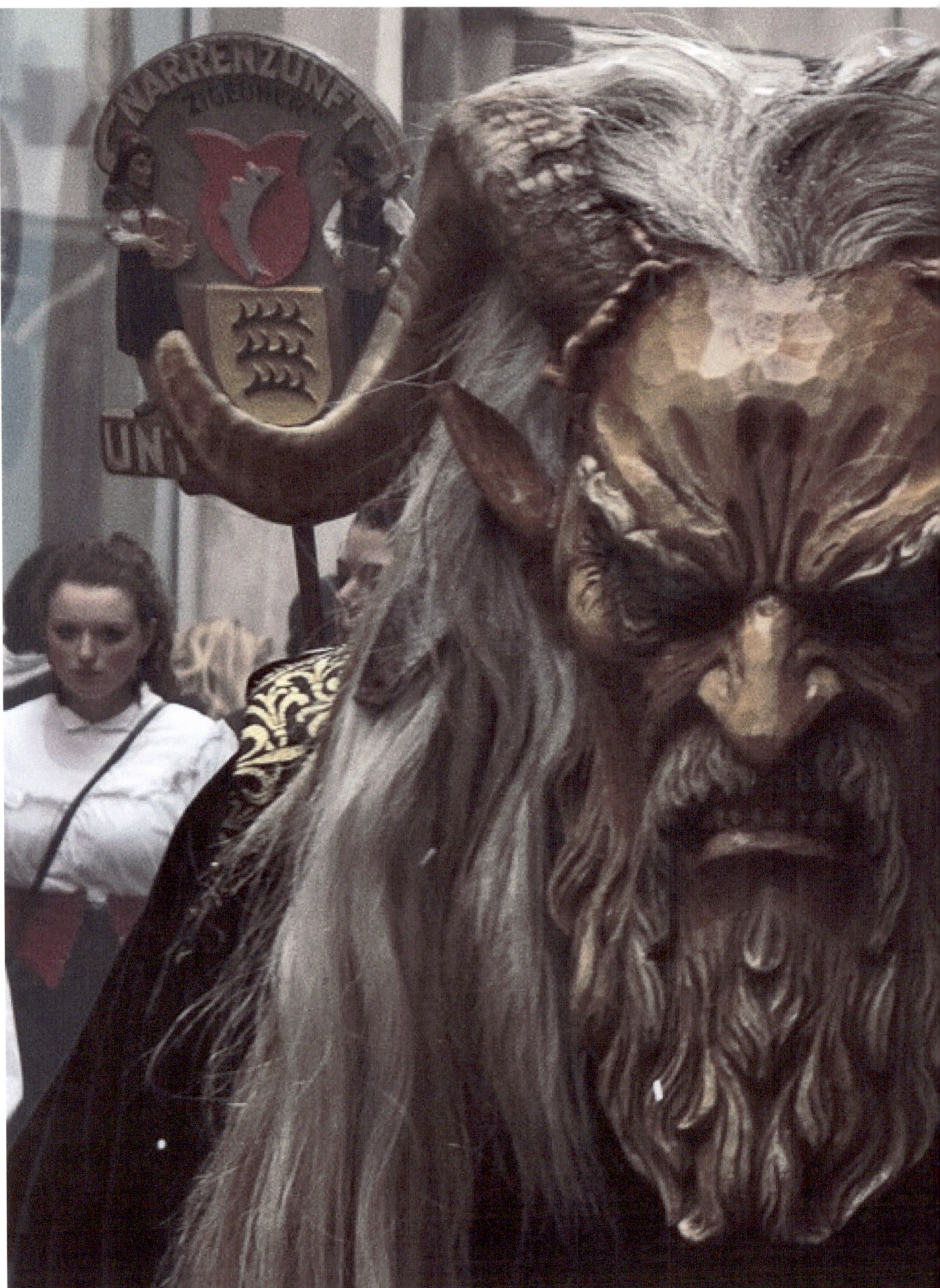

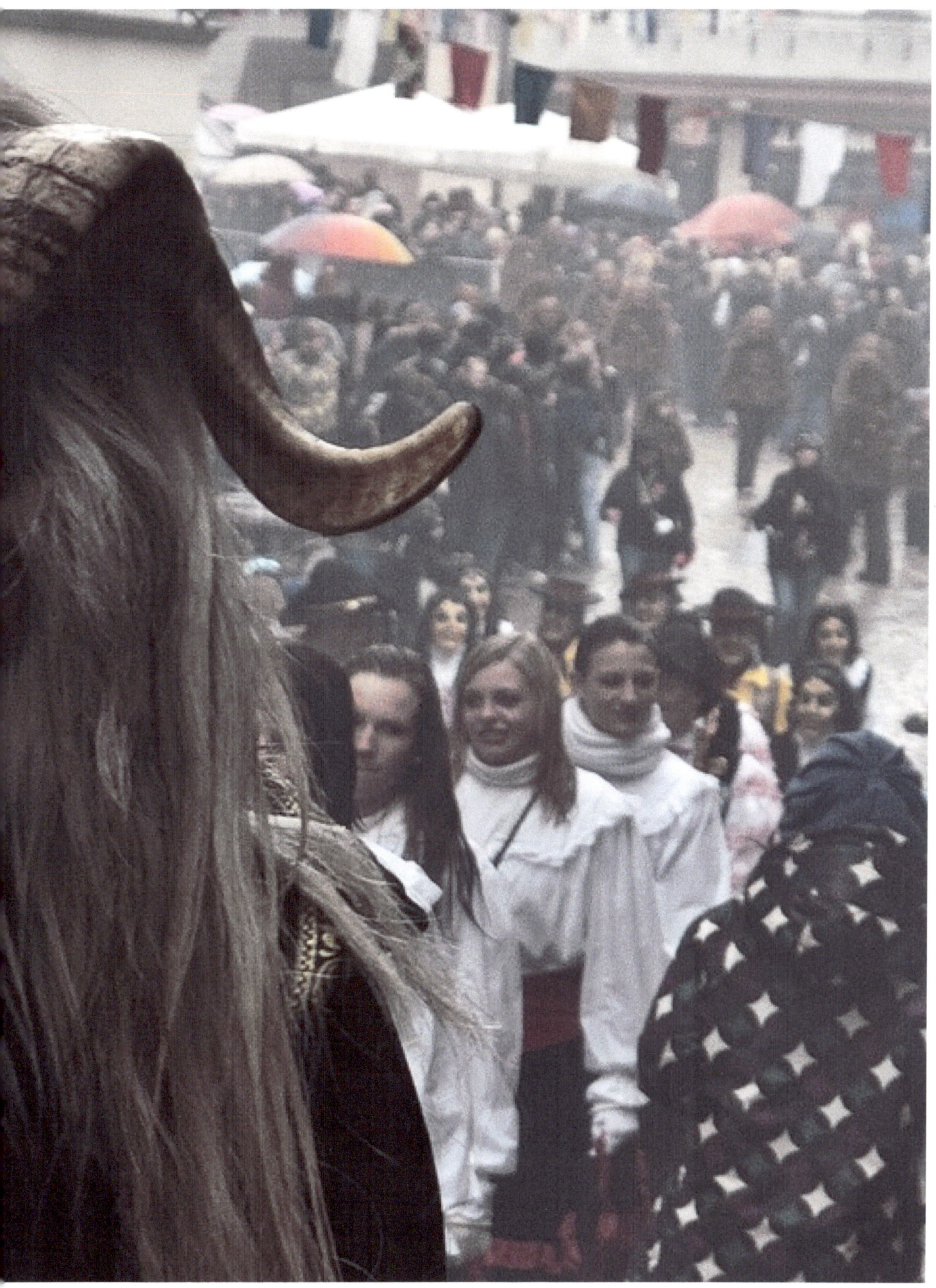

HUMAN

January 2015

Credits:

NOT for sale: human trafficking, Ira Gelb

Graffiti Monster Eating Human, epSos .de

Lost Humans, martin

human rights day, Catching.Light

the most human color, Gonzalo Díaz Fornaro

spotting my blind spot , Gisela Giardino

Bambi, Georgie Pauwels

Eternal Sunshine of the Spotless Mind, Gisela Giardino

Doug Anderson, "Blind Spot", 1983 , Phil Manker

Pepita... (56/365), Suedehead

Dirty Martini Howl 7, David Shankbone

Dirty Looks Greg Pianka - Bass , Ted Van Pelt

smile, Manish Bansal

keep smiling, pira7ex

The Masks of Fasching, LenDog64

Cover: Oslo Science Museum, Praktyczny Przewodnik